STOP ME BEFORE I EAT AGAIN!

LAYING IT ON THE LINE

Top O. The Morning!

HOG-WILD ABOUT QUILTING

BUSINESS IS BROOMING

Waiting for Santa

BEWARE OF THE SCARECROWS

Short and Sweet

4

5

LOVE ONE ANUDDER

GOOD MOOS TRAVELS FAST!

HERD IT ON THE RADIO

Cattle Mooran

Moosic Lover

Cow Swee

THE GRASS IS ALWAYS GREENER ... ON THE UDDER SIDE

The Grass Is Always Greener...On The Udder Side

15

COUNT YOUR BLESSINGS

TOMORROW IS ANUDDER DAY

17

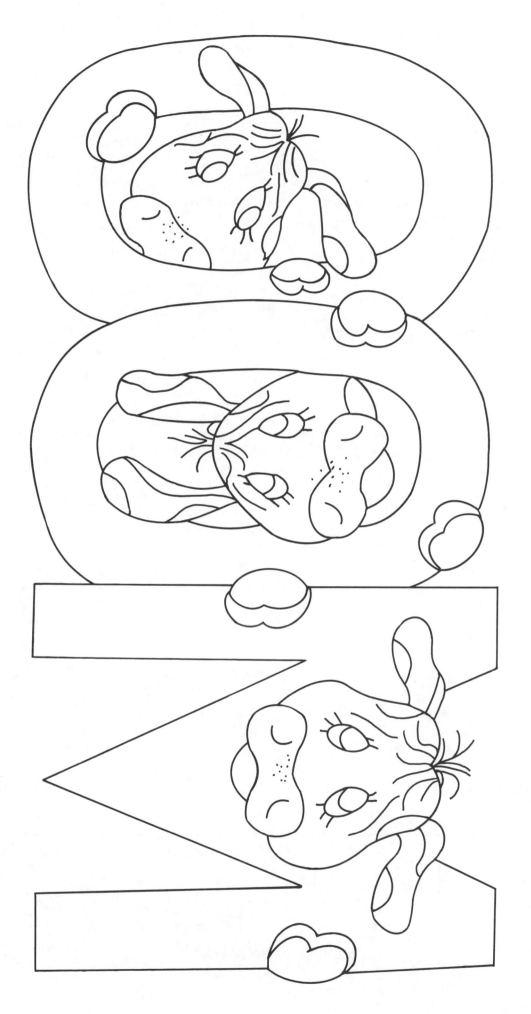

Moo

THINGS THE LITTER IT'S THE THAT COUNT...

LIFE IS SHORT... PIG OUT!

23

Love Me Tender

25

High On The Hog

27

28

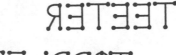

Teeter Toddler   Sugar Cured

Test Transfer

PAPAW'S LITTLE ANGEL

MEMAW'S LITTLE ANGEL

30

Memaw's Little Angel   Papaw's Little Angel

 PURR AND THE WORLD
PURRS WITH YOU

31

BLESSED ARE
THE PURR IN HEART

32

SUNNY SIDE UP

Sunny Side Up

LAYING IT ON THE LINE

BEWARE OF THE SCARECROWS

TRICK OR TREAT...WITCH WILL IT BE?

36

BROOMING
BUSINESS IS

Business Is Brooming

38

Broom Where You Are Planted

BROOM
WHERE YOU ARE PLANTED

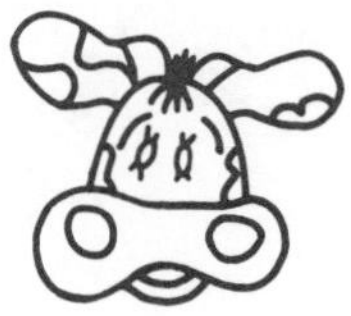

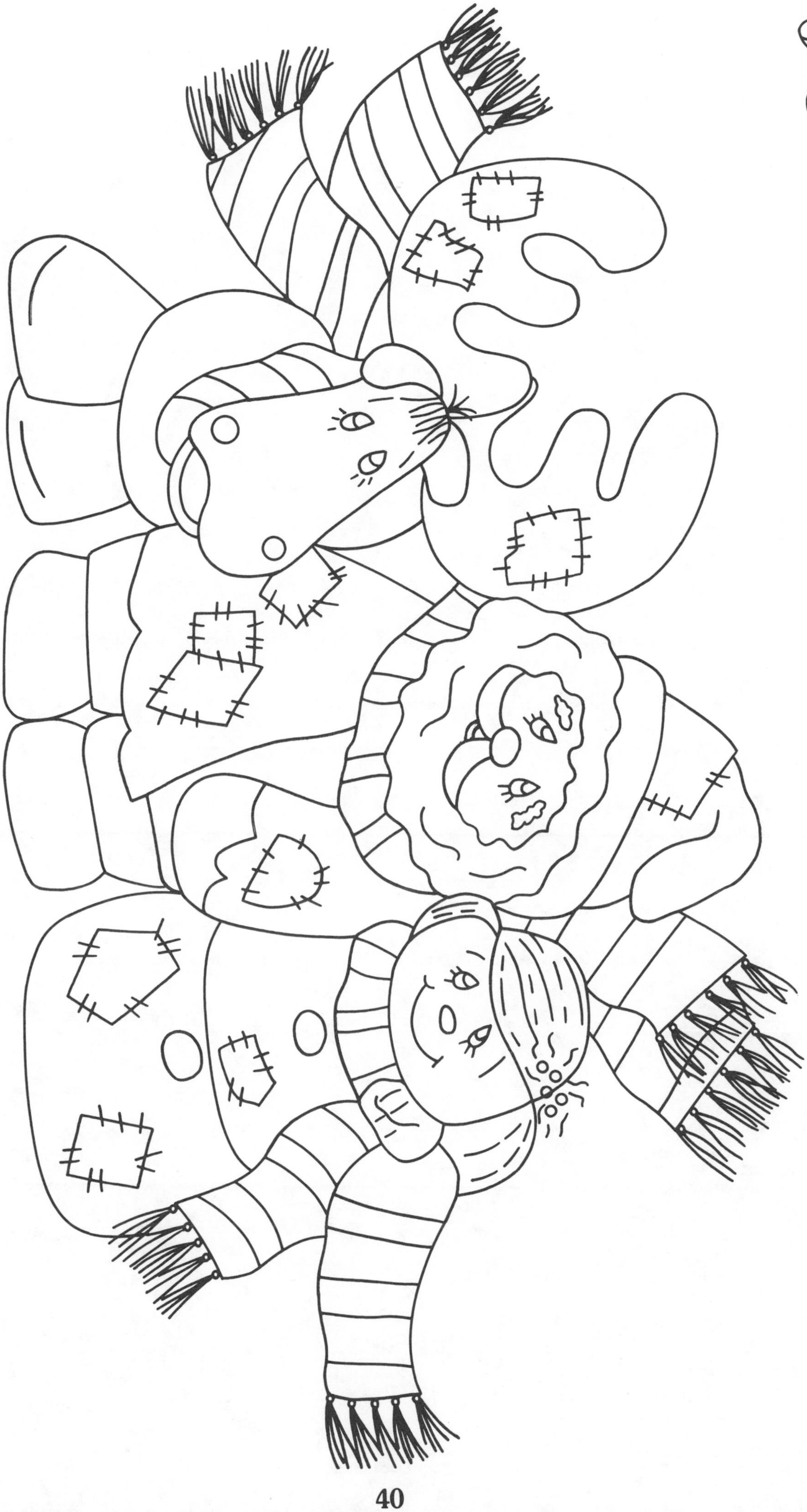

RUDOLPH WANNABE

41

MERRY KISSMOOSE

Merry Kissmoose

44

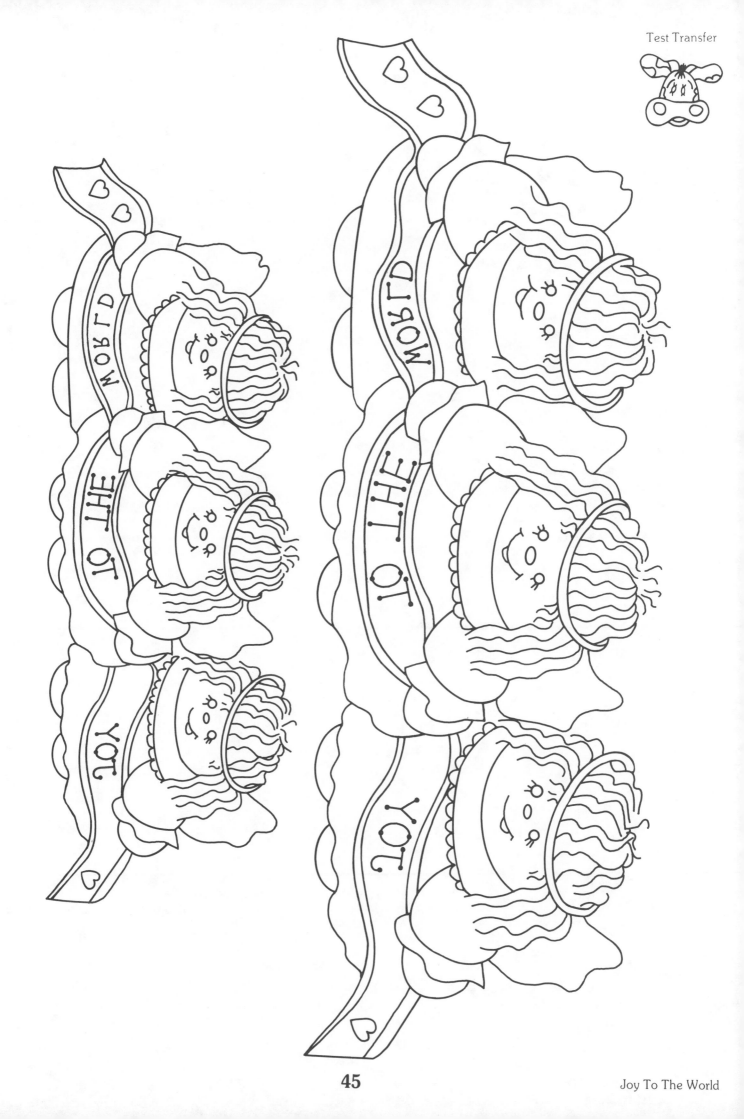

45

47

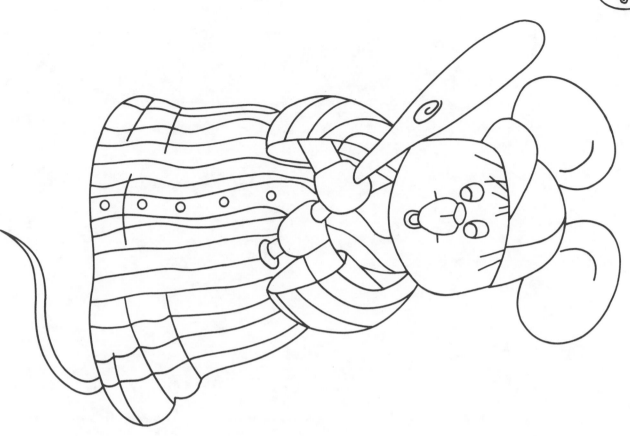

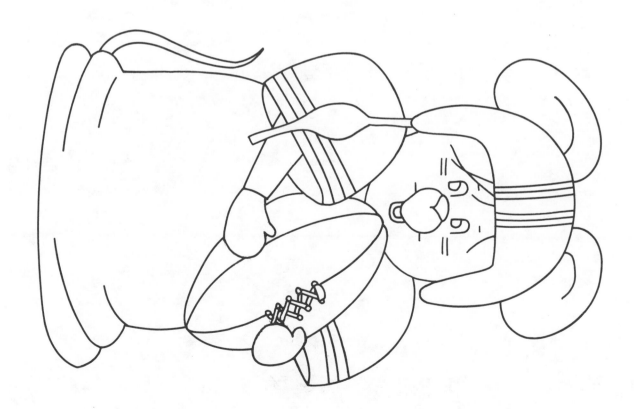

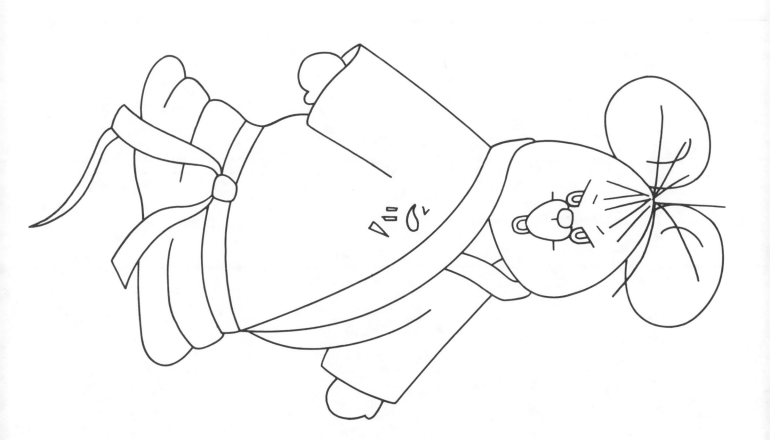

49

50

51

52

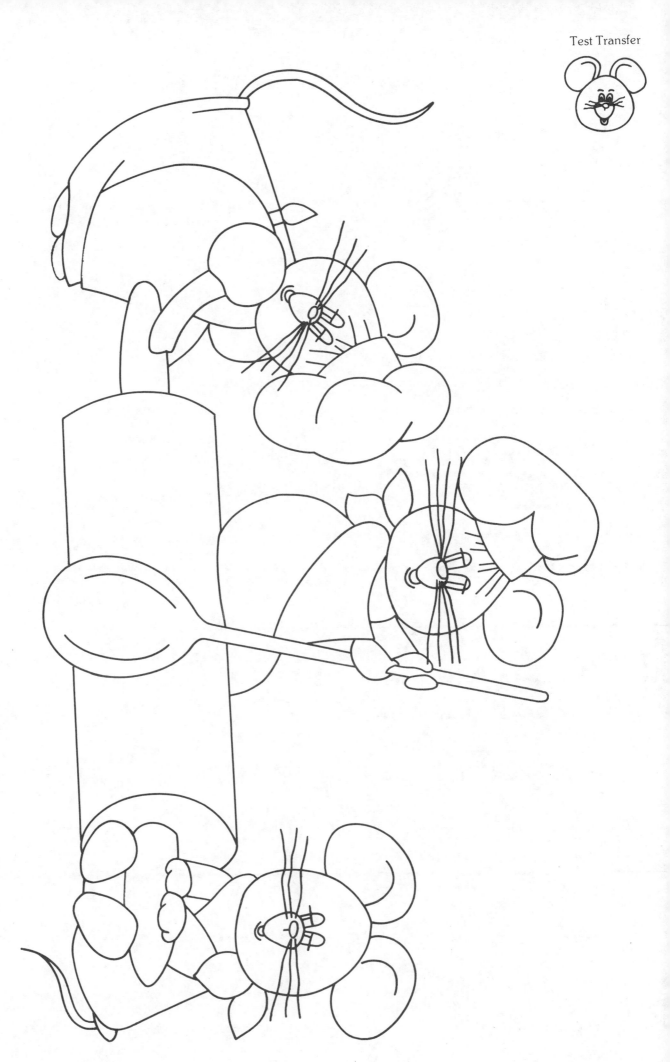

54

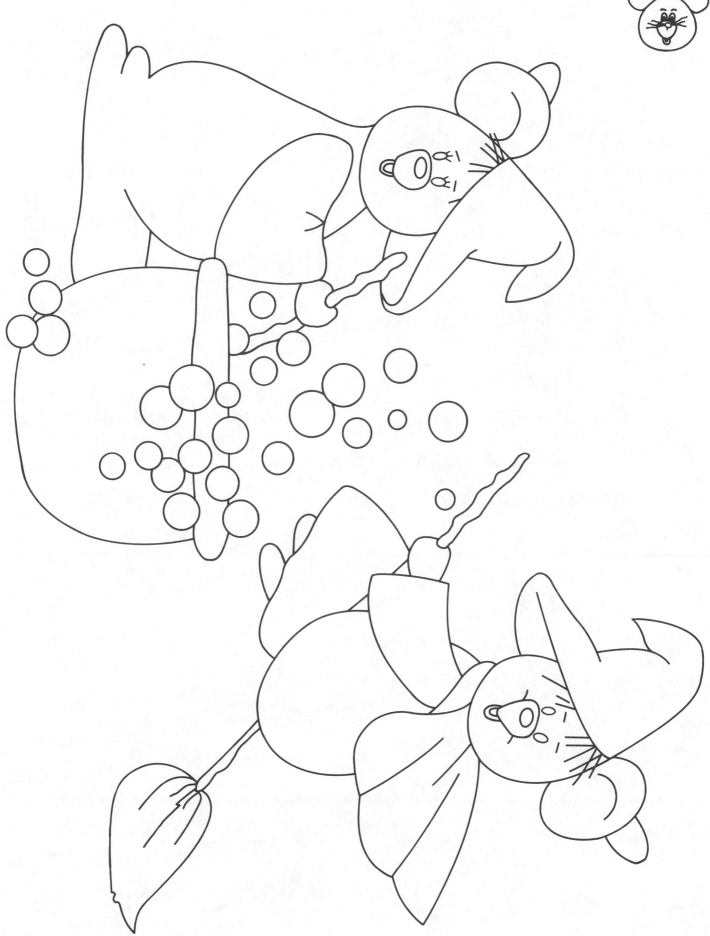

56

58

Christmas is Love

60

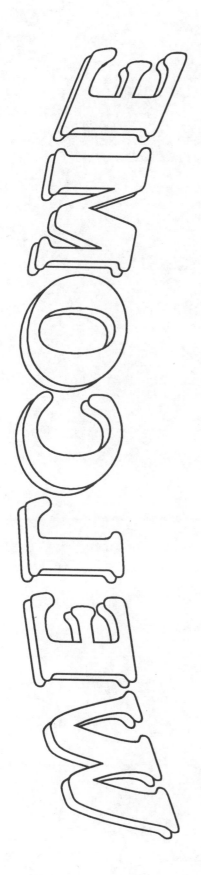

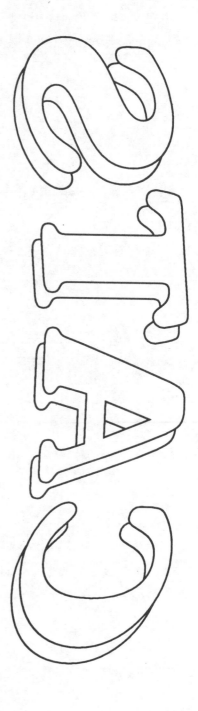

Cats Welcome

Test Transfer

I Love Kittens

63

I Love Kittens

I AM A CAT LOVER

I Am A Cat Lover

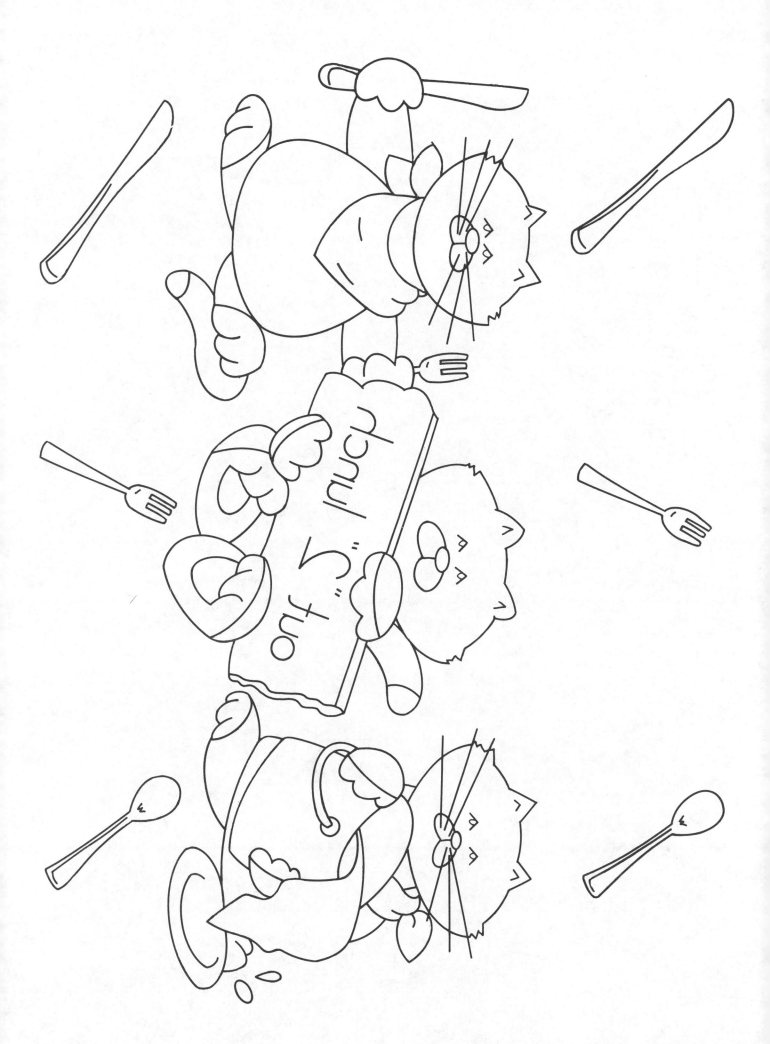

PUMPING IRON

Pumping Iron

HAPPINESS IS

A CHOCOLATE CHIP
COOKIE!

PAINTIN'
THE TOWN
RED

Paintin' The Town Red

Baby Sleeping

Baby Sleeping

Grandma's Little Girl

Grandma's Little Girl

Grandma's Little Man

Bless Your Heart

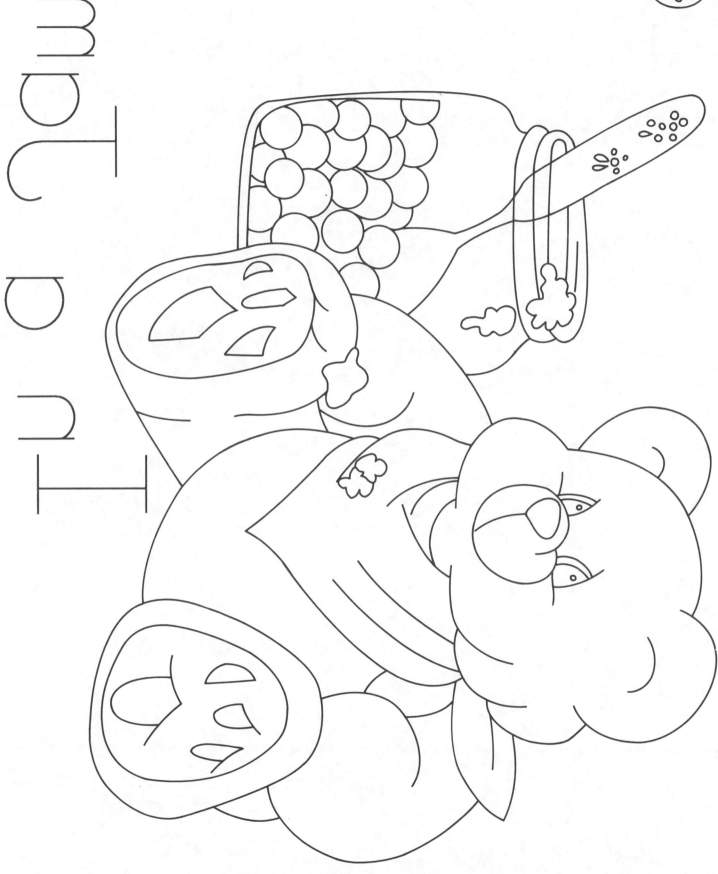

Tum Jam

In A Jam

Grade "A"

Teacher

Grade "A" Teacher

It's A Sew Sew Day

Hearts For Sale

84

Test Transfer

85

Go Ahead

Make My Day

87

Go Ahead

Make My Day

It's All About Attitude

89

bear

I Never Met A Meal I Didn't Like!

I like

91

Who's Been Eating My Porridge?

Thread Bear

Thread Bear

96

Who? Me?

98

Count Your Blessings

Count Your Blessings

106

107

Man's Best Friend

EGGS 5¢

FARM FRESH

Hello! Sunshine

Color Me Happy

113

Let Your Light Shine!

Let your light
Shine!

115

Sunshine Factory

Love Lights The World

119

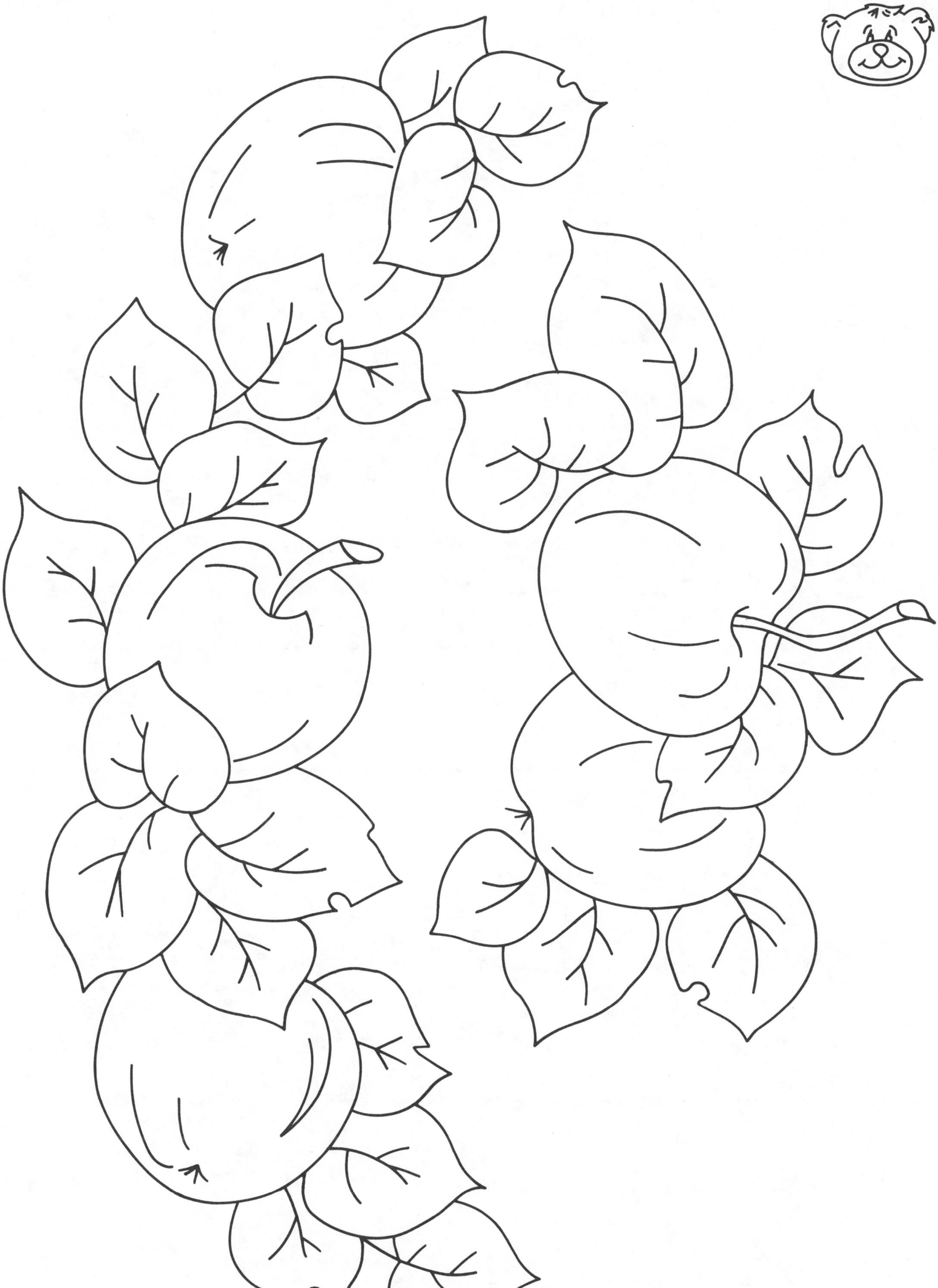

121

Get A Grip!

SPOOKS

125

Yo...Boo!

rock 'n roll is here to stay

Rock N' Roll Is Here To Stay

127

Bunny Hop

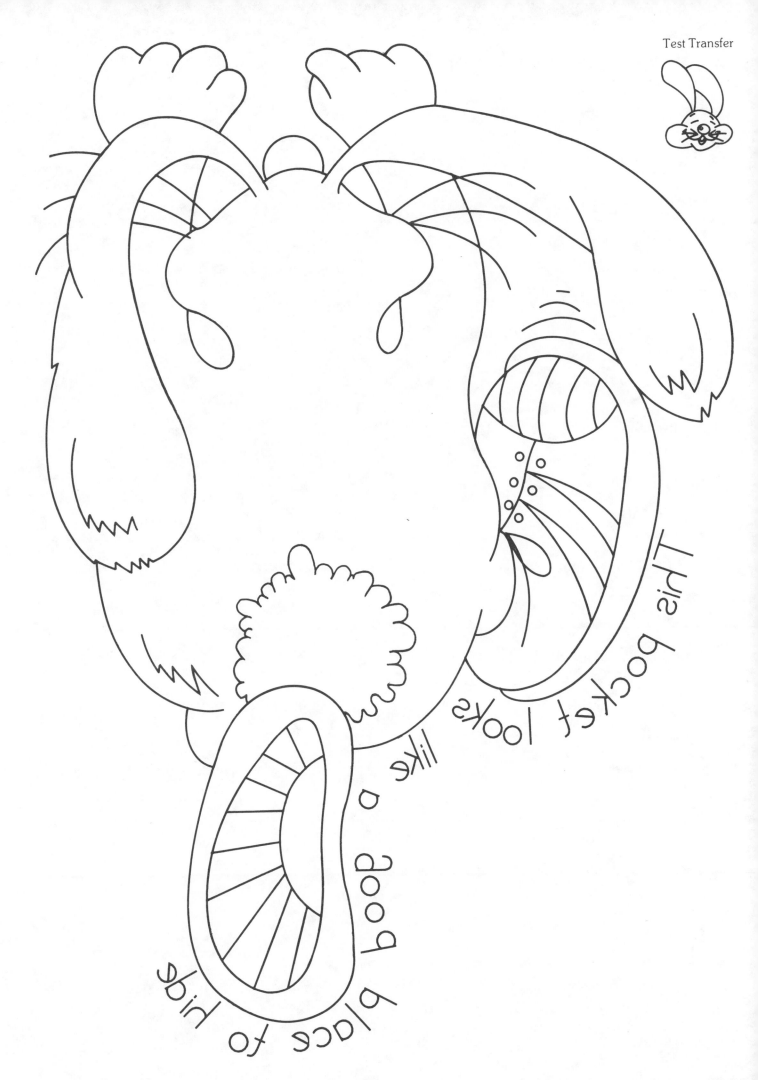

This Pocket looks like a good place to hide

This Pocket Looks Like A Good Place To Hide

Love your mother

130

Love Your Mother

Test Transfer

132

136

137

an apple a day

Plant A Tree

139

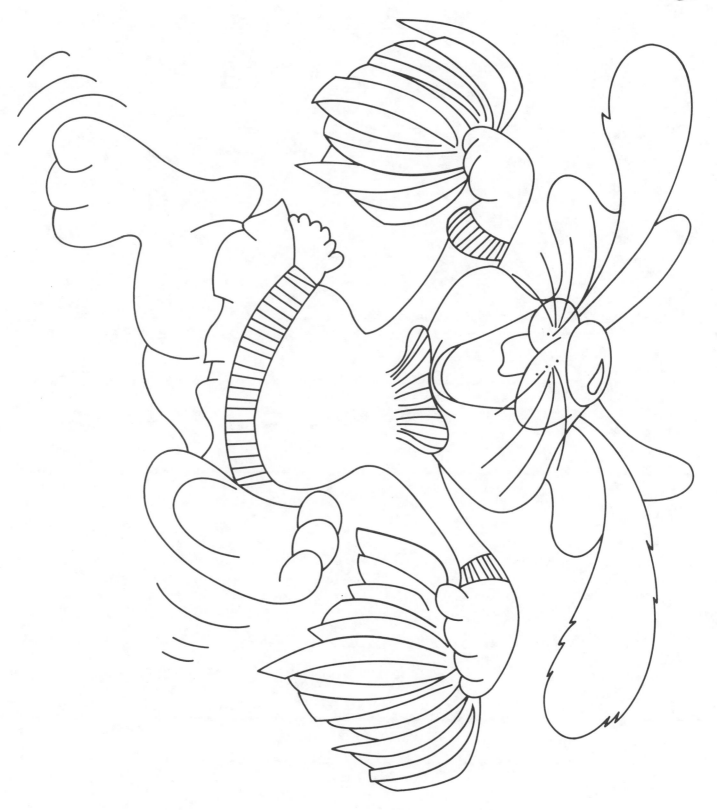

141

Bunny Ballerina

142

Bunny Ballerina

143

Jogging is my life!

Jogging is my Life!

Jogging Is My Life!

Downhill Racer

witchy wabbit

Witchy Wabbit

A Spooktacular Halloween

149

It's Wabbit Season

It's Turkey Time

It's Turkey Time

Christmas Treats

Merry Kissmoose

Jingle Bell

154

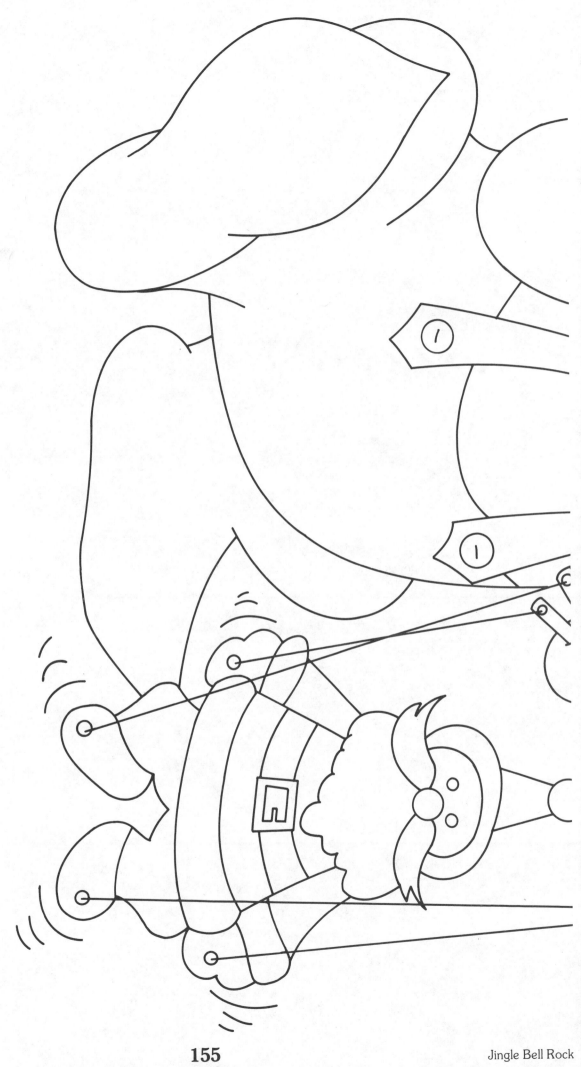

155

159

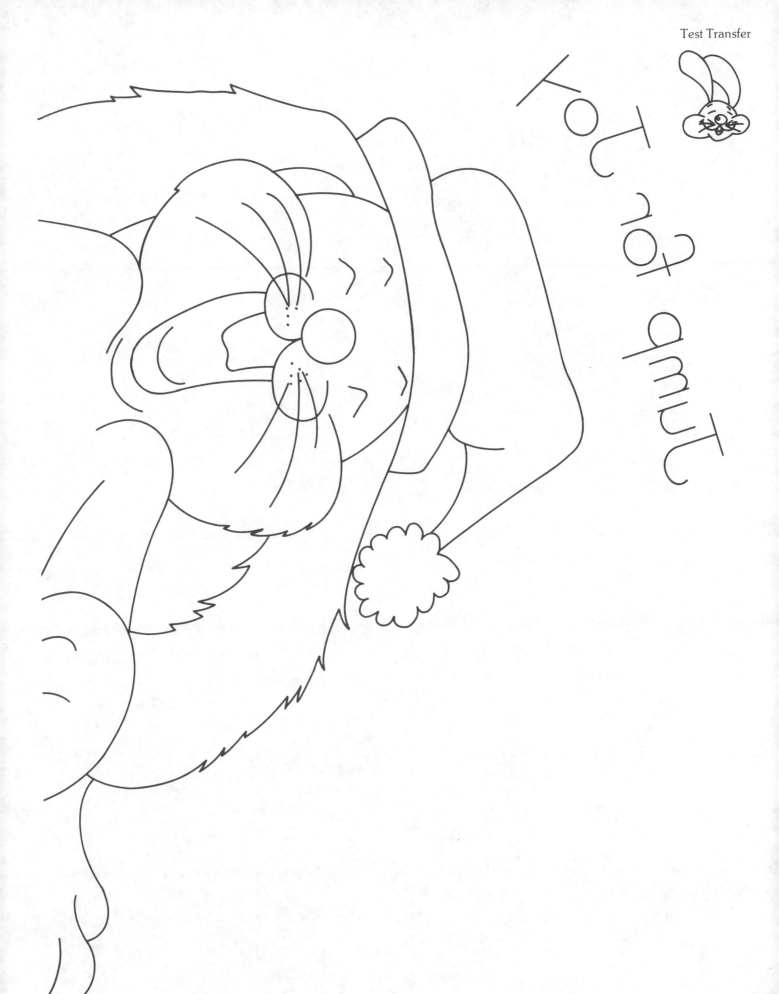

Jump for Joy

It's Christmas!

Jump For Joy

Test Transfer

SAVE OUR OCEANS

162

Save Our Oceans

163

Dolphin Safe

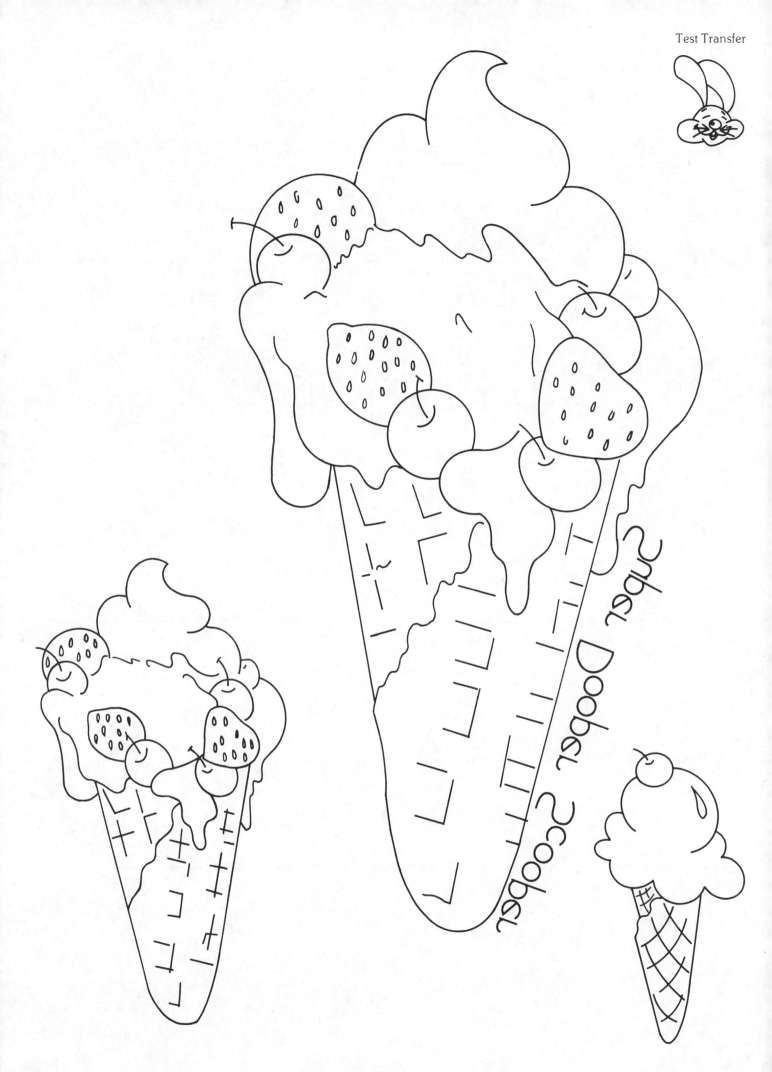

Super Dooper Scooper